This Book Belongs To
_____

Text and Illustrations Copyright © Dave Thorne 2020
Illustrations by Kris Lillyman 2020
Moral rights asserted

The right of Dave Thorne and Kris Lillyman to be identified as the Author and Illustrator of this work has been asserted by them in accordance with the Copyright, Design and Patents Act 1988.

All rights reserved. No part of this publication may be reproduced, stored in a retrieval system, or transmitted, in any form, or by any means (electronic, mechanical, photocopying, recording or otherwise) without the prior written permission of the publisher.

DORIS
The Fastest Chicken In The West

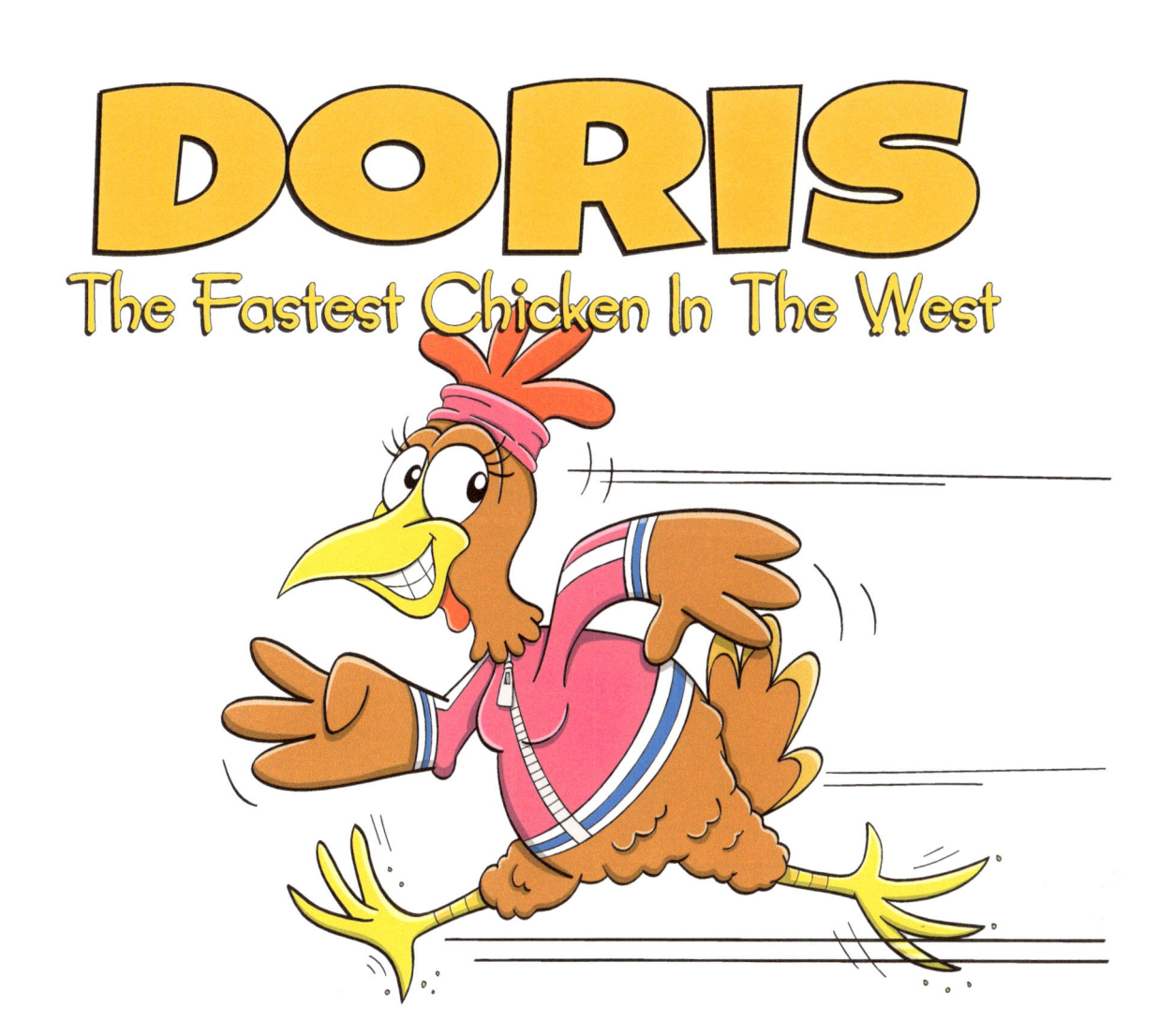

Written by Dave Thorne

Illustrated by Kris Lillyman

Doris was a chicken. There's nothing odd in that
But Doris could run blooming fast — much quicker than the cat
I'm sure if she was able, she still would never fly
You'll see she doesn't need to, when you see her flashing by.

She beat the goose; the duck; and pigs, which wasn't very hard
She even beat the farmers dog at running round the yard
She isn't odd in any way – no longer legs or feet
But pumping legs so very fast makes her hard to beat

She was challenged by the sheep and goat, and even by the llama
She beat them very easily, and even beat the farmer
Though farmer said it was unfair, he recently had eaten
But he lost again that afternoon, and Doris stayed unbeaten

Donkey tried to have a go, as fast as he could plod
But halfway round he felt so tired he had a little nod
Hare said he was busy, though was really saving face
He'd not want to get beaten – like when tortoise won their race

Now farmer had a good idea, while thinking in pyjamas
They'd have a farmyard running race with all the local farmers
They could bring their quickest animal – of any shape or size
And see who was the quickest, and win a special prize.

He sent a note through Owl-post to save a little cost
Then sent them through the postman, as Owl kept getting lost
He got a lot of entries to take part in the race
Thirty-two had entered – from all around the place.

With fifteen dogs; a cow; a goat; and a tabby cat
A sheep; a goose; a horse; a swan; and a scruffy rat
Then a cockerel wandered in. A very snooty bird
"My name" he said so proudly "is Lionel Partington the Third"

Doris was a quiver, and found it hard to speak
As Lionel stood tall over her, peering down his beak
"Hello. My name is Doris" Was all that she could say
As Lionel sniffed and turned his head, and rudely walked away

Doris was quite nervous. She'd heard that he was quick
She'd butterflies in her tummy, and felt a little sick
"He's fit" said Doris sadly. "I guess I'm coming second"
"We don't like him. He's a twit" is what the others reckoned.

SCORE BOARD

**FINAL RACE:
DORIS vs LIONEL**

FINISHING POST

Doris won her races, which cheered her up no end
They had to run one race again as pig crashed on a bend
The races that she wasn't in, well they were won by Lionel
So it worked out after seven heats, she'd meet him in the final.

Just before it started, he met her with a grin
"I'm really sorry little one. I know that I will win"
"I'm much too big, and strong for you – exceptionally fast"
"So, you may as well not bother as you know you're coming last"

Doris was so cross that she said something quite unkind
"I don't mind if I follow you. You look better from behind"
The Squirrel, who was referee, gave a little smirk
He hoped that Lionel wouldn't win - as he was a berk.

He called them up on to the line, and a whistle he did blow
And shouted very loudly "On your marks. Now get set. GO!"
Lionel shot off first of all. He was so very fast
It looked like he'd win easily, with Doris coming last.

But Doris fought so bravely, and ran with all her strength
Though halfway round Lionel led by just about a length
Then Doris overtook him, and burst into the lead
Lionel was quite shocked at that. She was quite fast indeed.

Doris started pulling clear, so Lionel had to cheat
He reached out with his nearest wing
and knocked her off her feet.
The crowd went "Boooo" – well wouldn't you?
It wasn't very fair
But Lionel laughed and ran ahead.
He really didn't care.

Doris got up – angry now and shot off in a hurry
Lionel saw her angry face, and he started to worry
He didn't think she'd pass him – and that she'd win the race
But more so that she'd catch him up
and slap his handsome face.

Doris started catching up. There wasn't far to go
And Lionel started getting tired, and he started to slow
The crowd were going wild right now - making such a din
Loudly urging Doris on, willing her to win.

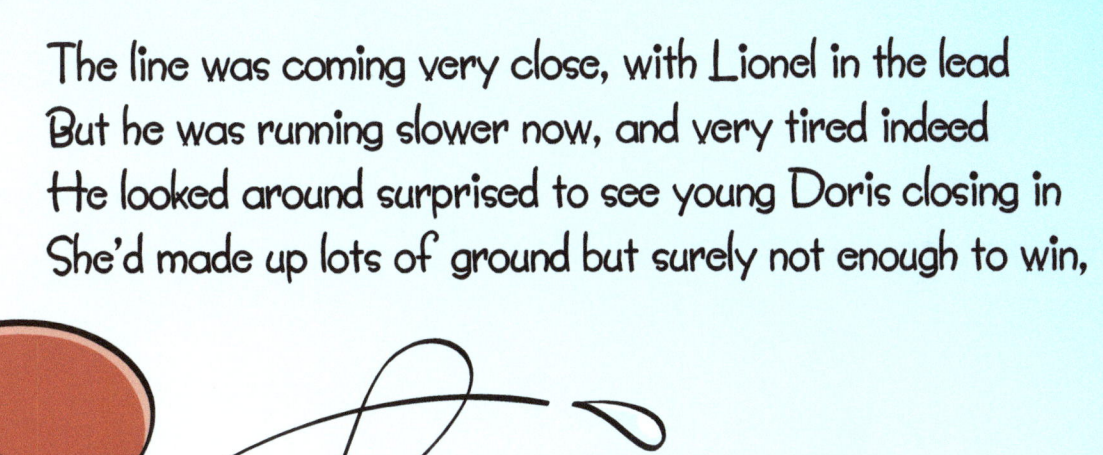

The line was coming very close, with Lionel in the lead
But he was running slower now, and very tired indeed
He looked around surprised to see young Doris closing in
She'd made up lots of ground but surely not enough to win,

Now Brian the naughty Turkey had watched all of the race
He didn't like what Lionel did and pulled a grumpy face
"I'll teach him not to cheat like that" the naughty turkey said
"I'll have to slow him down a bit, so Doris wins instead"

"This way to the line →"

He'd have to think quite quickly now
to stop the rooster winning
"I have a plan to sort him out!"
he said while slyly grinning
He took out farmers
fountain pen, and drew up
a new sign
And he held it high above
his head, saying
"This way to the line"

PRIVATE PROPERTY

Lionel saw it instantly, and changed his own direction
Not a clever thing to do, he might think on reflection
But his brain was very tired now, and struggling to think
His legs and feet were hurting, and was thirsting for a drink.

But the way the sign had sent him
was truly off the course
Right past the cows; round the pig;
and straight under the horse
He hadn't realised he'd gone wrong,
and that was all because
He kept on looking backwards
just to see where Doris was.

At last he finally realised that he'd run right off the track
When he ran right into Donkey, who was chewing on a snack
He bounced off Donkeys bottom, then tripped upon a bunny
And fell in piggy's trough, which Donkey thought quite funny.

Doris kept on running, until she'd won the race
She got a hug from farmer –
tears rolling down his face
"Doris won. Hip-hip hooray"
he shouted very loud
To clapping; hoots; and cheers aloud
from all the farmyard crowd.

The farmer got the silver trophy, a cup with gleaming handles
He'd used up all the money he was meant to spend on sandals
He handed it to Doris, but she couldn't pick it up
So she climbed up on a handle – and sat right in the cup.

As for naughty Lionel, well – he grumpily walked away
He's kept away from Doris ever since that famous day
And next time when the race was on, he chose not to compete
He knew he'd lose to Doris, or that he'd have to cheat.

So if you're driving by the farm, you may think you're mistaken
You're driving very fast but then you're quickly overtaken
Don't feel too bad. It's not your fault. I'm sure you tried your best
But you just lost to Doris. The fastest chicken in the west

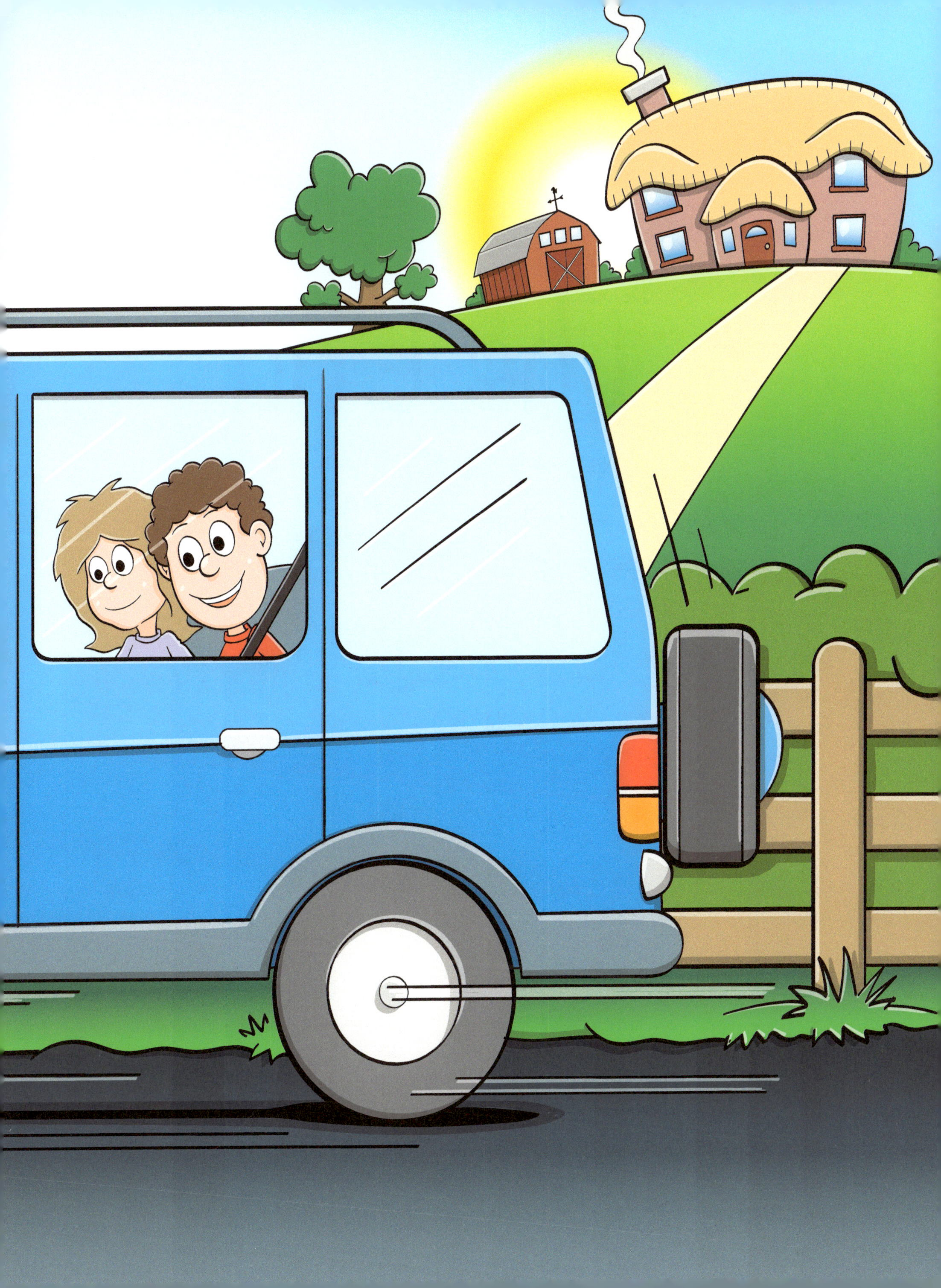

The End